DATE		

SHELTERING BOOKS
CHARITIES STARTED BY KIDS!
BY MELISSA SHERMAN PEARL AND DAVID A. SHERMAN

Published in the United States of America by Cherry Lake Publishing
Ann Arbor, Michigan
www.cherrylakepublishing.com

Reading Adviser: Marla Conn MS, Ed., Literacy specialist, Read-Ability, Inc.

Photo Credits: Photos used with permission from Sheltering Books, Cover, 1, 17, 21;
© Rawpixel.com / Shutterstock.com, 5; © Monkey Business Images / Shutterstock.com, 7;
© wavebreakmedia / Shutterstock.com, 9; © VGstockstudio / Shutterstock.com, 11; © Artem
Oleshko / Shutterstock.com, 13; © CoolR / Shutterstock.com, 15; © mattomedia Werbeagentur /
Shutterstock.com, 19

**LIBRARY OF CONGRESS CATALOGING-IN-PUBLICATION DATA HAS BEEN
FILED AND IS AVAILABLE AT CATALOG.LOC.GOV**

Cherry Lake Publishing would like to acknowledge the
work of The Partnership for 21st Century Learning. Please
visit *www.p21.org* for more information.

Printed in the United States of America
Corporate Graphics

SHELTERING BOOKS

CONTENTS

HOW DO THEY HELP?

READING IS FUNDAMENTAL

Not being able to read is devastating. Reading is not only fun but also a big part of learning. The better you can read, the more successful you can be.

Twenty-two percent of Americans have minimal reading **literacy**. They can't read beyond a third-grade level. They don't know the big words they need to know as adults.

Most children learn to read between the ages of 4 and 6 years old.

THINK!

Think about your own experiences learning to read. Do you feel that having other people to help you made it easier? Was it nice to have a variety of books to choose from?

5

This makes getting a job difficult. This can lead some families to homelessness. Many homeless families will end up in a shelter, often with just the basics. Studies show that 75 percent of homeless children struggle reading. This makes succeeding in school more difficult.

Sheltering Books is an organization that donates books to homeless shelters, **domestic violence** shelters, and **residential treatment centers** that house

In America, 1 in 50 children will be homeless at some time in their life.

THINK!

Think about what it would be like to live in a shelter. Do you think having books would make it a little easier? What other things would you like to have at the shelter?

7

children. Learning to read will help break the cycle of homelessness. With more books available to them, the greater the chances the kids there will be able to practice and start to love reading.

The ability to read is one of the most important skills a person can have.

MAKE A GUESS!

Sheltering Books has donated lots of books to homeless shelters, domestic violence shelters, and residential treatment centers. Are you able to guess how it collects all those books?

BOOKS NEED HOMES, TOO

From a very young age, Mackenzie Bearup wanted to help people. In 2003, when she was 10, she was diagnosed with complex regional pain syndrome (CRPS). There is no known cause or cure for this disease. Mackenzie was in pain all the time. The doctors tried different medicines to make her feel better. When one of

One of Mackenzie's first projects was to collect shoe donations to give to a women's shelter.

her doctors asked if there was anything that made her feel better, Mackenzie said, "Reading!"

While that wasn't exactly what the doctor meant, it was Mackenzie's truth. There is even a name for it: **bibliotherapy**.

Her doctor found this to be inspiring! She asked Mackenzie for help. The doctor was involved with a shelter for severely **abused** children. The shelter had built a library for the kids but didn't have any books for the

Reading took Mackenzie to far away worlds where she could meet amazing characters.

LOOK!

Look online or at
the library to find
pictures of shelters
with libraries. Are
they filled with books?
How do you think
the shelters that have
books are helping
the people who stay
there?

shelves. Of course, Mackenzie had a lot of books. She donated all her used books to the shelter. Then she asked her family, friends, and neighbors to donate and to spread the word.

A local newspaper published a story that sparked a ton of donations. Mackenzie was able to fill the shelter's library with 11,000 books.

Even though the library was full, Mackenzie kept receiving book donations.

The Library of Congress in Washington, D.C., holds more than 34 million books.

LOOK!

Look online or at the library to find out how many people are not able to read. How do you think this affects people's way of life?

15

She reached out to an organization in Atlanta, Georgia, that could help her give the books to other shelters. She then discovered that homeless kids were more likely to drop out of school and remain homeless.

Mackenzie developed a **strategy**. The books she'd be giving would help families develop a love of reading together. This would help kids stay in school. They'd graduate and maybe earn a college **scholarship**. What better way to break the cycle of homelessness?

In 2013, the average American adult spent about 5.5 hours reading a week.

ASK QUESTIONS!

What issues do you think families living in shelters might face? Ask a teacher or parent what they think. How might you be able to help?

17

SHELTERING BOOKS GROWS

Since 2006, Sheltering Books has been providing books to people who need them. At 23 years old, Mackenzie has been responsible for collecting and donating more than 360,000 books.

Mackenzie is still dealing with the pain of CRPS. Since it sometimes keeps her in bed for longer than she'd like, her younger brothers now help with her **philanthropy**.

Over the last 10 years, Mackenzie has, on average, collected nearly three books every single day.

Does Sheltering Books collect books in your area? Do you know anyone who has donated books to help people?

Not only do her brothers help with heavy lifting, but they also help count and sort the books by subject and age.

Mackenzie Bearup is a girl who gets things done. If there is a need, she works to find a solution. Then, when her job is complete, she'll take a seat, pull out a book, and read.

Sheltering Books needs to be sure books are sorted correctly. Different shelters, treatment centers, and overseas soldiers get different books.

CREATE!

Show what making a difference looks like. Place a box in your classroom and collect gently used books from your classmates. Then find a local shelter where you can donate them.

21

GLOSSARY

abused (uh-BYOOZD) harmed or treated unkindly

bibliotherapy (bib-lee-oh-THER-uh-pee) the use of reading to make an illness bearable

domestic violence (duh-MES-tik VYE-uh-luhns) the use of physical force to harm a family member

literacy (LIT-ur-uh-see) the ability to read and write

philanthropy (fuh-LAN-thruh-pee) helping others by giving time or money to causes or charities

residential treatment centers (rez-ih-DEN-shuhl TREET-muhnt SEN-turz) mental health facilities where medical professionals help the patients who live there until they are better

scholarship (SKAH-lur-ship) a sum of money or other aid given to a student because of merit or need, to continue his or her studies

strategy (STRAT-ih-jee) a plan or method for achieving a specific goal or result

FIND OUT MORE

WEB SITES

www.childrn.org
Children's Restoration Network offers programs that help homeless children receive food, school supplies, adult guidance, scholarships, and more.

www.dosomething.org/us/facts/11-facts-about-literacy-america
Discover facts about literacy from DoSomething.org, a global movement of young people making positive changes.

www.powerofpain.org/rsd-crps
Learn some facts about CRPS from the International Pain Foundation.

www.shelteringbooks.org
Learn more about Sheltering Books and what it does.

INDEX

ABOUT THE AUTHORS

David Sherman and Melissa Sherman Pearl are cousins who understand and appreciate that you don't have to be an adult to make a difference.